D1403233

The Fan in the Can

Mary Elizabeth Salzmann

Consulting Editor, Diane Craig, M.A./Reading Specialist

Published by ABDO Publishing Company, 4940 Viking Drive, Edina, Minnesota 55435.

Printed in the United States.

Credits
Edited by: Pam Price
Curriculum Coordinator: Nancy Tuminelly
Cover and Interior Design and Production: Mighty Media
Photo Credits: AbleStock, Corbis Images, Hemera, Photodisc, Wewerka Photography

Library of Congress Cataloging-in-Publication Data

Salzmann, Mary Elizabeth, 1968-
      The fan in the can / Mary Elizabeth Salzmann.
          p. cm. -- (First rhymes)
      ISBN 1-59679-479-8 (hardcover)
      ISBN 1-59679-480-1 (paperback)
        1. English language--Rhyme--Juvenile literature. I. Title. II. Series.

PE1517.S3526 2005
808.1--dc22
                                                                            2005048029

SandCastle™ books are created by a professional team of educators, reading specialists, and content developers around five essential components that include phonemic awareness, phonics, vocabulary, text comprehension, and fluency. All books are written, reviewed, and leveled for guided reading and early intervention reading, and designed for use in shared, guided, and independent reading and writing activities to support a balanced approach to literacy instruction.

Let Us Know

After reading the book, SandCastle would like you to tell us your stories about reading. What is your favorite page? Was there something hard that you needed help with? Share the ups and downs of learning to read. We want to hear from you! To get posted on the ABDO Publishing Company Web site, send us e-mail at:

sandcastle@abdopub.com

SandCastle Level: Beginning

can

fan

man

pan

van

Look at the  .

This is a .

See the .

Look at the  .

This is a  .

The can is silver.

The fan is pretty.

The man is happy.

The pan is new.

The van is big.

The Fan in the Can

Jan has a new fan.

16

Jan puts the fan
in a big can.

Jan puts the can
with the fan
in a frying pan.

Jan gives the pan
with the fan
in the can
to Dan the man.

Dan the man
puts the pan
with the can
and the fan
in his tan van!

About SandCastle™

A professional team of educators, reading specialists, and content developers created the SandCastle™ series to support young readers as they develop reading skills and strategies and increase their general knowledge. The SandCastle™ series has four levels that correspond to early literacy development in young children. The levels are provided to help teachers and parents select the appropriate books for young readers.

Emerging Readers
(no flags)

Beginning Readers
(1 flag)

Transitional Readers
(2 flags)

Fluent Readers
(3 flags)

These levels are meant only as a guide. All levels are subject to change.

ABDO
Publishing Company

To see a complete list of SandCastle™ books and other nonfiction titles from ABDO Publishing Company, visit www.abdopub.com or contact us at: 4940 Viking Drive, Edina, Minnesota 55435 • 1-800-800-1312 • fax: 1-952-831-1632